String Time Joggers

14 pieces for flexible ensemble

Kathy and David Blackwell

Contents

T0088271

Sea Suite

1. Shark attack! 2
2. Barrier Reef 4
3. Cap'n Jack's Hornpipe 6

Jazz Suite

4. Simple syncopation 8
5. Feelin' blue 9
6. Broadway or bust 10

Jamaican Suite

7. Tinga Layo 12
8. Jamaican lullaby 14
9. Kingston Calypso 15

Hollywood Suite

10. Spy movie 2 18
11. Sad movie 20
12. Action movie 22

Extras

13. Cowboy song 24
14. Banuwa 24

1 o 15 This symbol indicates the CD track numbers for each piece. The top number indicates the complete performance, and the bottom number the accompaniment alone. A tuning note (A) is located on track 29.

Violin

Sea Suite

1. Shark attack!

© Oxford University Press 2007

Printed in Great Britain

OXFORD UNIVERSITY PRESS, MUSIC DEPARTMENT, GREAT CLARENDON STREET, OXFORD OX2 6DP

The Moral Rights of the authors have been asserted. Photocopying this copyright material is ILLEGAL.

22
B
p
cresc.
f
p
cresc.
f
26
p
cresc.
f
p
cresc.
f
30
C
f
mf
f
mf
35
dim.
p
dim.
p
39
cresc.
ff
cresc.
ff

2
16
2. Barrier Reef
Very calm ♩ = 60
1
2
4
mp
pizz.
9
13
A
arco
17
21
poco rall.
B
a tempo
pizz.

26

30
dim.
p
pp
dim.
p
pp

3
17
3. Cap'n Jack's Hornpipe
Lively ♩ = 84
1
2
3
3
f
f
9
15
21
A
2
2
mf
28
B
mf

34
3
3
42
C
f
f
47
52
58
rall.
ff
ff

Jazz Suite

4. Simple syncopation

Happy ♩ = 112

1

2

6

10

A

14

18

B

23

5 ○ 19

5. Feelin' blue

Slow and moody ♩ = 68

1

2

2

2

𝄋

mp

div.

mp

6

Fine

11

A

f

unis.

f

15

D.S. al Fine

6
20
6. Broadway or bust
Bright swing ♩ = 112
1
2
3
mf
7
12
17
A
f
23

29
B
pizz.
p
pizz.
p
35
arco
f
41
C
arco
f
45
49
rit.
ff
ff

7
21
7. Tinga Layo
(Part 1 and Harmony)
West Indian Trad.
Happy ♩ = 126
1
HARMONY
4
mf
7
A
f
11
B
17
22
C
mp
26

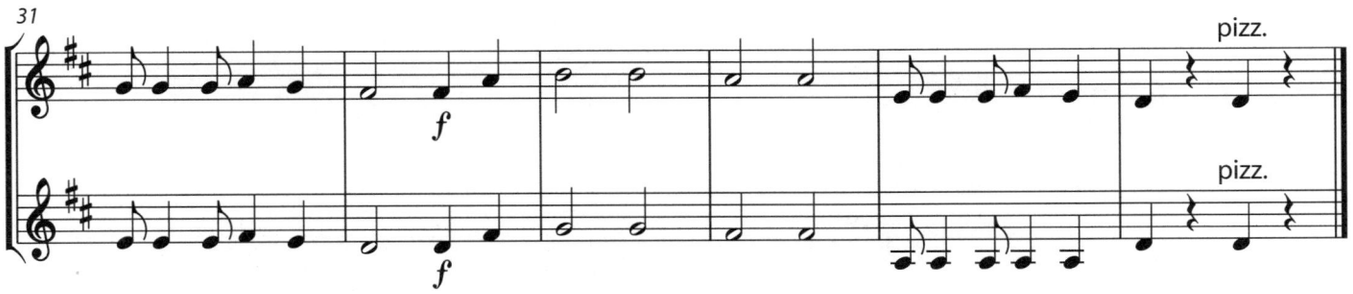

7. Tinga Lago

(Part 2)

West Indian Trad.

8
22
8. Jamaican lullaby
Jamaican Trad.
Gently flowing ♩ = 104
DESCANT
1
2
4
mp
8
A
13
mf
17
dim.
mp

9
23
9. Kingston Calypso
(Part 2)
Sunny ♩ = 130
2
4
mf
9
A
15
21
B
26
C
mp
31
36
D
3
f
43

9
23
9. Kingston Calypso
(Part 1 and Harmony)
Sunny ♩ = 130
1
HARMONY
4
mf
8
13
A
18
B
23

28
C
mp
mp

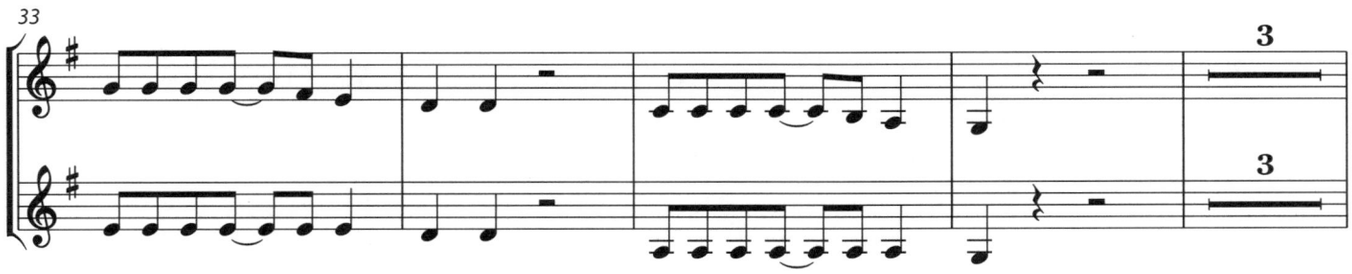
33
3
3

40
D
f
f

44

10 ○ 24

10. Spy movie 2

Menacing ♩ = 130

1

2

pizz.

p

pizz.

p

8

A

4

arco

f

4

arco

f

16

20

B

25

mp

mp

30
C
ff
ff
mp
mp
35
39
p
p
2
2
pizz.
pizz.
p
p

SPY MOVIE
2

11
25
11. Sad movie
Gently flowing ♩ = 88
1
2
4
p
8
12
3
A
mp
18
22
B
mf

27
32
C
f
f
37
rit.
a tempo
D
4
4
dim.
dim.
mp
mp
45
50
rit.
slower
p
p

12 ○ 26
12. Action movie
Marching ♩ = 112
1
2
3
f
7
11
A
mp
16
cresc.
f
21
B

25
C
29
pizz.
mp
pizz.
mp
33
cresc.
arco
f
cresc.
arco
f
37
D
41
3
ff
3
ff

Extras

13. Cowboy song

MELODY

With a swagger ♩ = 100

1

6

12

OSTINATO

HARMONY 1 2

div.

last time

2

14. Banuwa

MELODY

African Trad.

Gently ♩ = 84

1

4

OSTINATO

2